Assessing the Democratic Party's Commitment to America's Values

Brayan Quinonez

Published by Brayan Quinonez, 2023.

Thanks to my little brother S

Introduction:

A Historical Perspective: The Democratic Party's Alignment with American Values.

Introduction:

Understanding the historic context of the Democratic Party's alignment with American values is integral for comprehending its dedication to upholding core standards at some point of history. This in-depth evaluation delves into the party's evolution, inspecting its position in advancing key American beliefs such as freedom, equality, and justice. By exploring landmark Democratic policies and legislation, we intention to check the party's historic music report and its alignment with American values.

The Democratic Party's Origins:

The Democratic Party traces its origins again to the Democratic-Republican Party, established via Thomas Jefferson and James Madison in the early years of the United States. Jeffersonian democracy emphasised character liberties, confined government, and the empowerment of the frequent citizen, aligning with the concepts enshrined in the American founding documents.

Jacksonian Democracy and the Expansion of Democracy:

The emergence of Jacksonian Democracy in the 1820s and 1830s marked a widespread length in Democratic Party history. Led with the aid of Andrew Jackson, the celebration championed the growth of suffrage to white male citizens, difficult the prevailing elitism of the time. This push for broader democratic participation mirrored a dedication to the crucial American fee of equality and the proper to political representation.

Civil Rights and Racial Equality:

The Democratic Party's historic alignment with American values can be considered thru its position in advancing civil rights and racial equality. In the mid-20th century, Democratic President Lyndon B. Johnson signed landmark civil rights legislation, which includes the Civil Rights Act of 1964 and the Voting Rights Act of 1965. These transformative legal guidelines aimed to dismantle racial segregation and make sure equal rights for all citizens, aligning with America's values of justice and equality.

Social Security and Economic Security:

The Democratic Party has additionally performed a large function in merchandising financial protection and social welfare. President Franklin D. Roosevelt's New Deal policies, carried out all through the Great Depression, blanketed the institution of Social Security, which supplied a protection internet for retirees and prone populations. This dedication to financial protection displays the Democratic Party's alignment with American values of compassion, community, and the pursuit of the frequent good.

Healthcare Access and Affordable Care:

The Democratic Party's pursuit of available healthcare in addition exemplifies its alignment with American values. The passage of the Affordable Care Act (ACA) below President Barack Obama aimed to enlarge get entry to to healthcare, defend people with pre-existing conditions, and enlarge insurance to tens of millions of Americans. This initiative displays the party's dedication to the ideas of fairness, equality, and the faith that fine healthcare must be reachable to all.

Labor Rights and Workers' Protections:

Throughout history, the Democratic Party has recommended for labor rights and workers' protections, aligning with the American cost of honest cure and the pursuit of financial opportunity. Democratic administrations have supported insurance policies such as minimal wage increases, place of job protection regulations, and the safety of collective bargaining rights. These efforts display a dedication to fostering a honest and equitable society that upholds the dignity and rights of workers.

Women's Rights and Gender Equality:

The Democratic Party has been at the forefront of advertising women's rights and gender equality. From the suffrage motion to the battle for reproductive rights, Democratic leaders and legislators have championed insurance policies aimed at advancing gender equality and making sure equal possibilities for women. These efforts align with the American values of freedom, equality, and the pursuit of justice for all.

LGBTQ+ Rights and Inclusion:

The Democratic Party has proven a dedication to LGBTQ+ rights and inclusion, reflecting the American values of equality and acceptance. Democratic administrations and lawmakers have supported initiatives such as marriage equality, anti-discrimination laws, and the safety of LGBTQ+ individuals' rights. These efforts exhibit the party's alignment with the ideas of fairness, respect, and the pursuit of equal rights for all Americans.

Environmental Stewardship and Climate Change:

In latest years, the Democratic Party has more and more targeted on environmental stewardship and addressing local weather change. Efforts to fight local weather exchange and promote renewable electricity align with the American fee of accountable stewardship of the herbal world. The party's help for global local weather agreements and the merchandising of sustainable insurance policies display a dedication to keeping the surroundings for future generations.

Rethinking and Adapting to Evolving Values:

As American values and societal priorities have developed over time, so too has the Democratic Party. It has validated a willingness to adapt and reply to altering instances and the moving desires of the American people. This flexibility and openness to revolutionary trade mirror the party's dedication to ultimate aligned with the evolving values of a dynamic and various nation.

Conclusion:

A historic standpoint displays the Democratic Party's alignment with American values at some stage in its existence. From its roots in Jeffersonian democracy to its advocacy for civil rights, financial security, social welfare, and equal rights, the birthday party has persistently championed values such as freedom, equality, justice, and opportunity. Understanding this alignment is vital for comprehending the party's dedication to the standards that shape the basis of American society and its ongoing efforts to uphold and enhance these values in an ever-changing world.

Democratic Party Platform: A Closer Look at Key Values and Priorities.

Introduction:

The Democratic Party's platform serves as a guidepost for its coverage agenda and displays the party's core values and priorities. This in-depth evaluation takes a nearer appear at the key values and priorities of the Democratic Party platform. By analyzing unique coverage proposals and initiatives, we intention to supply a complete appreciation of the party's imaginative and prescient and its alignment with the values and aspirations of the American people.

Inclusivity and Social Justice:

The Democratic Party platform emphasizes inclusivity and social justice as necessary values. It seeks to create a society that respects and values the dignity and really worth of all individuals, irrespective of their race, gender, sexual orientation, religion, or socioeconomic status. The birthday celebration promotes insurance policies aimed at combating systemic discrimination, advancing equal rights, and fostering a extra equitable society.

Economic Opportunity and Fairness:

Economic probability and equity are central issues in the Democratic Party platform. The birthday party advocates for insurance policies that promote upward mobility, limit earnings inequality, and furnish equal get entry to to monetary opportunities. This consists of initiatives such as growing the minimal wage, increasing get entry to to lower priced training and job training, and assisting small companies and entrepreneurship.

Affordable Healthcare and Public Health:

The Democratic Party locations a robust emphasis on inexpensive healthcare and public health. It seeks to make certain that each American has get entry to to quality, lower priced healthcare, and helps initiatives such as increasing Medicaid, strengthening the Affordable Care Act (ACA), and reducing the fee of prescription drugs. The birthday party additionally prioritizes public fitness initiatives, addressing troubles such as intellectual health, opioid addiction, and the prevention of infectious diseases.

Climate Change and Environmental Protection:

The Democratic Party platform acknowledges the urgency of addressing local weather alternate and defending the environment. It advocates for insurance policies that promote smooth energy, minimize carbon emissions, and transition to a sustainable economy. The celebration helps worldwide local weather agreements, invests in renewable electricity infrastructure, and promotes conservation efforts to shield herbal assets and fight environmental degradation.

Education and Access to Knowledge:

The Democratic Party is dedicated to increasing get admission to to schooling and knowledge. It promotes insurance policies that intention to make pleasant training lower priced and handy from early childhood thru university and beyond. The birthday party helps elevated funding for public schools, increasing get admission to to early childhood education, investing in trainer education and expert development, and lowering the burden of pupil mortgage debt.

Criminal Justice Reform and Public Safety:

The Democratic Party platform advocates for crook justice reform and the advertising of public safety. It seeks to tackle systemic troubles inside the crook justice system, such as mass incarceration and racial disparities. The birthday party helps initiatives that emphasize neighborhood policing, limit obligatory minimal sentences, promote rehabilitation and reintegration, and tackle the root reasons of crime.

Immigration and Diverse Communities:

The Democratic Party values the contributions of immigrants and goals to create a honest and humane immigration system. It helps complete immigration reform, inclusive of a pathway to citizenship for undocumented individuals, safety for DACA recipients, and reforms to family-based and employment-based immigration policies. The celebration additionally promotes insurance policies that guard the rights and dignity of diverse communities and condemns discrimination and hate crimes.

Women's Rights and Gender Equality:

The Democratic Party is committed to advancing women's rights and reaching gender equality. It helps insurance policies that promote equal pay for equal work, shield reproductive rights, increase get admission to to low priced childcare, and fight gender-based violence. The birthday party additionally works to promote women's management and illustration in all areas of society, together with politics, business, and the judiciary.

Gun Violence Prevention:

The Democratic Party platform acknowledges the want for complete gun violence prevention measures. It helps commonsense reforms such as expanding heritage checks, closing loopholes in gun sales, and stopping men and women with a records of home violence or intellectual sickness from gaining access to firearms. The celebration advocates for insurance policies that stability Second Amendment rights with public protection considerations.

International Relations and Global Cooperation:

The Democratic Party emphasizes the significance of global family members and world cooperation. It promotes diplomacy, multilateralism, and worldwide cooperation to tackle international challenges such as local weather change, nuclear non-proliferation, human rights, and financial inequality. The birthday party helps global alliances and partnerships to foster peace, stability, and development on a world scale.

Conclusion:

The Democratic Party's platform displays its key values and priorities, addressing a broad vary of problems from social justice to monetary opportunity, healthcare, local weather change, education, crook justice reform, immigration, women's rights, gun violence prevention, and worldwide cooperation. By intently analyzing the party's platform, we achieve a complete perception of its imaginative and prescient for America and its dedication to developing a extra inclusive, fair, and affluent society. While unique insurance policies and priorities can also evolve over time, the Democratic Party's platform serves as a roadmap for its ongoing efforts to align its insurance policies with the values and aspirations of the American people.

Criticisms and Counterarguments: Assessing the Democratic Party's Commitment to America's Values.

Introduction:

As a distinguished political celebration in the United States, the Democratic Party has confronted its honest share of criticisms involving its dedication to America's values. This in-depth evaluation examines the criticisms leveled in opposition to the celebration and affords counterarguments to examine its dedication to upholding core American principles. By delving into these criticisms and counterarguments, we intention to provide a complete assessment of the Democratic Party's dedication to America's values and the complexities surrounding political discourse.

Criticism: Government Overreach and Excessive Regulation:

One frequent criticism of the Democratic Party is the understanding of authorities overreach and immoderate regulation. Critics argue that Democratic policies, such as environmental policies and healthcare mandates, infringe upon private liberties and stifle financial growth. Counterarguments contend that these insurance policies are critical to shield public health, fight local weather change, and make certain equal get right of entry to to healthcare, aligning with America's values of well-being, justice, and the frequent good.

Criticism: Fiscal Responsibility and National Debt:

Some critics argue that the Democratic Party's spending proposals and social packages make contributions to an unsustainable countrywide debt and lack of fiscal responsibility. They contend that expansive authorities programs, such as conventional healthcare and free university tuition, area an undue burden on taxpayers and future generations. Counterarguments emphasize that investing in social applications can tackle monetary inequality, promote upward mobility, and reinforce the social fabric, reflecting America's values of fairness, equal opportunity, and social welfare.

Criticism: Second Amendment Rights:

Critics assert that the Democratic Party's stance on gun manage infringes upon Second Amendment rights assured by means of the Constitution. They argue that proposed gun manage measures, such as history tests and assault weapons bans, undermine the individual's proper to self-defense. Counterarguments emphasize the want for complete gun security measures to tackle the public fitness disaster of gun violence. They contend that smart guidelines can assist defend lives and promote public protection whilst respecting the rights of accountable gun owners.

Criticism: Immigration and Border Security:

Critics accuse the Democratic Party of prioritizing open borders and dismissing countrywide safety concerns. They argue that lenient immigration policies, such as help for pathways to citizenship and opposition to strict border enforcement, undermine America's sovereignty and put the u . s . a . at risk. Counterarguments stress the significance of complete immigration reform, balancing protection issues with compassion and cognizance of immigrants' contributions. They contend that the party's values of inclusivity, fairness, and humanitarianism are aligned with America's immigrant records and values.

Criticism: Cultural and Social Issues:

Critics regularly spotlight the Democratic Party's positions on cultural and social issues, maintaining that the celebration promotes values that are opposite to regular or conservative perspectives. They cite aid for LGBTQ+ rights, reproductive rights, and secularism as examples. Counterarguments emphasize the significance of person rights, diversity, and inclusion, arguing that America's values evolve over time and need to replicate the altering social panorama to make sure equal rights and social progress.

Criticism: Lack of Bipartisanship and Political Divisiveness:

Critics argue that the Democratic Party contributes to political divisiveness with the aid of failing to attain throughout the aisle and interact in bipartisan cooperation. They contend that the party's pursuit of its agenda at the price of compromise undermines the spirit of cooperation indispensable to high quality governance. Counterarguments keep that partisan gridlock regularly stems from ideological variations and opposition, and that the Democratic Party's dedication to its core values displays the democratic manner and the pursuit of a innovative agenda that aligns with America's values of justice, equality, and progress.

Criticism: Influence of Special Interest Groups:

Critics assert that the Democratic Party is unduly influenced by means of distinct pastime groups, such as labor unions and environmental organizations, which prioritize their very own agendas over the broader pursuits of the American people. They argue that this have an effect on skews policymaking and undermines the party's dedication to the frequent good. Counterarguments contend that pastime organizations play a necessary function in democracy, supplying illustration for quite a number constituencies and advancing insurance policies that promote social justice, workers rights, and environmental sustainability.

Criticism: Lack of Support for Law and Order:

Critics declare that the Democratic Party does now not prioritize regulation and order sufficiently, pointing to perceived leniency in crook justice reforms and the party's affiliation with actions advocating for defunding the police. They argue that this strategy undermines public security and disregards the rights of victims. Counterarguments stress the want for crook justice reform to address systemic troubles and promote fairness. They emphasize the significance of police accountability and community-based options to make sure public protection whilst respecting character rights, aligning with America's values of justice and equal safety underneath the law.

Criticism: Lack of Support for Small Businesses and Free Market:

Critics assert that the Democratic Party's policies, such as growing the minimal wage and advocating for employee protections, disproportionately burden small corporations and restrict free market dynamics. They argue that immoderate legislation and excessive taxes avert entrepreneurship and monetary growth. Counterarguments emphasize the significance of balancing financial policies with protections for workers, consumers, and the environment. They contend that Democratic insurance policies can create a fairer and extra sustainable economic system that advantages small businesses, workers, and society as a whole, aligning with America's values of fairness, opportunity, and a stage enjoying field.

Criticism: Lack of Transparency and Ethical Concerns:

Critics from time to time query the Democratic Party's transparency and moral conduct, pointing to allegations of political corruption, cronyism, and have an impact on peddling. They argue that such conduct undermines the party's credibility and its dedication to accurate governance. Counterarguments stress the want for robust moral standards, transparency, and accountability throughout all political parties. They hold that character instances of wrongdoing need to no longer overshadow the broader dedication to public carrier and the pursuit of the frequent good, aligning with America's values of integrity, fairness, and accountability.

Conclusion:

The Democratic Party's dedication to America's values has been challenge to a range of criticisms, reflecting the variety of views in political discourse. Evaluating these criticisms and counterarguments affords a nuanced perception of the complexities surrounding the party's policies, principles, and dedication to American values. While opinions may additionally differ, open speak and a crucial evaluation of these arguments make contributions to a extra knowledgeable and positive political landscape, facilitating growth towards a society that upholds the standards of justice, equality, opportunity, and the frequent good.

Democratic Party's Vision for America's Future: A Forward-Looking Assessment

Introduction:

As the Democratic Party appears in advance to America's future, its imaginative and prescient for the u . s . displays a dedication to shaping a prosperous, inclusive, and sustainable society. This in-depth evaluation explores the party's forward-looking policies, initiatives, and aspirations aimed at addressing rising challenges and opportunities. By inspecting the Democratic Party's imaginative and prescient for America's future, we intention to determine its dedication to core values and its potential to navigate the complexities of a hastily altering world.

Future-oriented Policies: Embracing Technological Advancements and Workforce Transformation

In an technology of fast technological developments and automation, the Democratic Party's imaginative and prescient for America's future includes insurance policies that equip folks with the competencies and assets critical to thrive in the digital age. We discover the party's dedication to advertising innovation, helping technological lookup and development, and making sure that technological developments advantage all Americans. By inspecting its forward-looking policies, we acquire insights into the party's dedication to fostering financial growth, job creation, and equitable opportunities.

Sustainable Development and Climate Action: A Greener Future for Generations to Come

The Democratic Party's imaginative and prescient for America's future encompasses a robust dedication to sustainable improvement and local weather action. We check the party's dedication to transitioning to smooth energy, mitigating the affects of local weather change, and developing a sustainable and resilient economy. By analyzing insurance policies and techniques aimed at addressing environmental challenges, merchandising renewable electricity sources, and lowering carbon emissions, we obtain insights into the party's imaginative and prescient for a greener future.

Education and Technology: Equipping Future Generations for the Digital Age

As science continues to seriously change more than a few components of society, the Democratic Party's imaginative and prescient for America's future consists of a focal point on training in the digital era. We discover insurance policies that promote equitable get admission to to pleasant education, guide innovation in instructional technologies, and tackle the digital divide. By evaluating the party's dedication to getting ready future generations for a technology-driven society, we achieve insights into its dedication to America's values of equal probability and know-how advancement.

Racial Equity and Social Cohesion: Building a Just and United Society

The Democratic Party's imaginative and prescient for America's future encompasses a robust dedication to racial fairness and social cohesion. We analyze insurance policies and initiatives aimed at dismantling systemic racism, merchandising range and representation, and fostering social concord throughout numerous communities. By inspecting the party's imaginative and prescient for a extra simply and united America, we consider its dedication to the core values of equality and unity.

Economic Opportunity and Inclusive Growth: Fostering Prosperity for All

The Democratic Party's imaginative and prescient for America's future consists of a dedication to financial chance and inclusive growth. We discover insurance policies aimed at lowering profits inequality, increasing get entry to to first-rate jobs, and promotion entrepreneurship. By evaluating the party's dedication to fostering financial prosperity for all

Americans, we obtain insights into its dedication to America's values of fairness, equal opportunity, and upward mobility.

Healthcare Access and Affordability: Ensuring Quality Care for All Americans

The Democratic Party's imaginative and prescient for America's future encompasses a dedication to available and lower priced healthcare. We determine insurance policies aimed at increasing get admission to to fine healthcare, lowering healthcare costs, and defending humans with pre-existing conditions. By inspecting the party's dedication to making sure that all Americans have get admission to to complete healthcare, we reap insights into its dedication to America's values of well-being and the pursuit of the frequent good.

Infrastructure and Sustainable Development: Modernizing America's Systems

The Democratic Party's imaginative and prescient for America's future consists of a center of attention on infrastructure and sustainable development. We discover insurance policies aimed at modernizing America's transportation, energy, and verbal exchange systems. By assessing the party's dedication to investing in infrastructure, advertising sustainable development, and growing jobs, we obtain insights into its dedication to fostering monetary growth, environmental stewardship, and extended first-rate of life.

Global Engagement and Diplomacy: America's Role in a Complex World

In an increasingly more interconnected world, the Democratic Party's imaginative and prescient for America's future consists of a dedication to worldwide cooperation, multilateralism, and diplomacy. We take a look at the party's strategy to world challenges, such as worldwide trade, human rights, and geopolitical stability. By evaluating its dedication to world engagement, we acquire insights into its dedication to America's values of peace, cooperation, and world leadership.

Science and Innovation: Harnessing Knowledge for Progress

The Democratic Party's imaginative and prescient for America's future consists of a focal point on science and innovation. We discover insurance policies that assist scientific research, promote technological advancements, and harness know-how for societal progress. By assessing the party's dedication to investing in lookup and development, we obtain insights into its dedication to America's values of know-how advancement, progress, and evidence-based decision-making.

Inclusive Democracy and Voting Rights: Strengthening Democratic Institutions

The Democratic Party's imaginative and prescient for America's future encompasses a dedication to inclusive democracy and defending vote casting rights. We look at insurance policies aimed at increasing get right of entry to to the ballot, lowering obstacles to voter participation, and strengthening democratic institutions. By evaluating the party's dedication to keeping and improving democratic processes, we attain insights into its dedication to America's values of fairness, representation, and the proper to self-governance.

Conclusion:

The Democratic Party's imaginative and prescient for America's future is a forward-looking roadmap that seeks to tackle rising challenges and construct a society that displays the nation's core values. Through a complete evaluation of the party's future-oriented policies, consisting of technological advancements, sustainable development, education, racial equity, monetary opportunity, healthcare, infrastructure, international engagement, science, and inclusive democracy, we acquire a holistic grasp of its dedication to America's values. While the party's imaginative and prescient may additionally evolve over time, its dedication to fostering a prosperous, inclusive, and sustainable society stays rooted in the concepts that have formed the nation. By significantly inspecting its forward-looking agenda, this e book affords readers with insights into the Democratic Party's imaginative and prescient for America's future and encourages considerate discussions on the course ahead for the nation.

Ensuring Equity and Social Justice: The Democratic Party's Commitment to a Fair Society

Introduction:

The Democratic Party has lengthy championed the reason of fairness and social justice as a central pillar of its imaginative and prescient for a honest and inclusive society. In this in-depth analysis, we delve into the party's dedication to making sure fairness and social justice, inspecting its insurance policies and initiatives aimed at dismantling systemic inequalities, merchandising social cohesion, and growing a society that upholds the values of equality, fairness, and chance for all Americans.

Tackling Systemic Racism: Advancing Racial Equity

The Democratic Party acknowledges that systemic racism persists in quite a number factors of American society. It is dedicated to addressing this problem via insurance policies and initiatives aimed at advancing racial equity. These encompass crook justice reforms to tackle racial disparities, investments in schooling to bridge the success gap, and monetary initiatives to promote wealth introduction in marginalized communities. By addressing the root reasons of systemic racism, the birthday party seeks to construct a society the place people of all races have equal get admission to to possibilities and can thrive.

Gender Equality and Women's Empowerment: Fostering Inclusive Opportunities

The Democratic Party is devoted to advertising gender equality and empowering female in all components of society. It advocates for policies that make sure equal pay for equal work, defend reproductive rights, and fight gender-based violence. The celebration additionally works to make bigger women's illustration in management positions and helps initiatives that supply girls with equal possibilities for profession advancement, education, and monetary success. By championing gender equality, the Democratic Party ambitions to create a society the place girls have the identical rights, opportunities, and employer as their male counterparts.

LGBTQ+ Rights and Inclusion: Championing Equal Treatment and Acceptance

The Democratic Party is a staunch recommend for LGBTQ+ rights and inclusion. It helps insurance policies that restrict discrimination based totally on sexual orientation and gender identity, advocates for marriage equality, and promotes get right of entry to to healthcare and social offerings for LGBTQ+ individuals. The celebration additionally works to create secure and inclusive environments for LGBTQ+ formative years in colleges and helps efforts to stop the damaging exercise of conversion therapy. By championing LGBTQ+ rights, the Democratic Party strives to create a society the place all individuals, regardless of their sexual orientation or gender identity, are accepted, respected, and protected.

Economic Equality and Fairness: Bridging the Wealth Gap

The Democratic Party acknowledges the developing wealth hole in America and is dedicated to promotion financial equality and fairness. It advocates for insurance policies that tackle earnings inequality, such as elevating the minimal wage, making sure truthful taxation, and enforcing modern tax reforms. The birthday celebration additionally helps get right of entry to to low-priced housing, healthcare, and schooling as imperative factors of financial security. By pursuing financial equality, the Democratic Party goals to create an equitable society the place humans have equal possibilities to prosper and succeed.

Affordable Housing and Urban Renewal: Creating Livable Communities for All

The Democratic Party acknowledges the significance of less costly housing and city renewal in growing shiny and inclusive communities. It helps insurance policies that make bigger get right of entry to to inexpensive housing, make investments in the revitalization of deprived neighborhoods, and promote sustainable city development. The birthday party additionally acknowledges the want to tackle housing discrimination and make certain that every person has a protected and secure location to name home. By prioritizing low-cost housing and city renewal, the Democratic Party ambitions to create communities the place persons of all backgrounds can live, work, and thrive.

Disability Rights and Inclusion: Ensuring Access and Opportunities

The Democratic Party is committed to advancing incapacity rights and inclusion. It helps insurance policies that shield the rights of people with disabilities, such as the Americans with Disabilities Act (ADA), and works to make sure equal get admission to to education, employment, transportation, and public services. The birthday celebration additionally advocates for multiplied funding for incapacity offerings and helps initiatives that promote inclusive and on hand communities. By championing incapacity rights and inclusion, the Democratic Party strives to create a society the place men and women with disabilities can totally take part and contribute.

Indigenous Rights and Tribal Sovereignty: Honoring Native American Communities

The Democratic Party acknowledges the special challenges confronted by way of Native American communities and is dedicated to honoring indigenous rights and tribal sovereignty. It helps insurance policies that recognize treaty obligations, enhance get right of entry to to healthcare and education, and promote monetary improvement in Native American communities. The celebration additionally works to tackle historic injustices and helps initiatives that hold and promote indigenous languages, cultures, and traditions. By upholding indigenous rights and tribal sovereignty, the Democratic Party targets to forge a stronger, greater inclusive state that honors the contributions of Native American communities.

Criminal Justice Reform: Ensuring Fairness and Rehabilitation

The Democratic Party acknowledges the want for complete crook justice reform to tackle systemic problems inside the justice system. It helps insurance policies aimed at lowering mass incarceration, ending obligatory minimal sentences, and merchandising picks to incarceration such as diversion packages and restorative justice. The birthday celebration additionally advocates for investments in rehabilitation and reentry packages to facilitate profitable reintegration into society. By advertising crook justice reform, the Democratic Party seeks to create a honest and simply gadget that focuses on rehabilitation, accountability, and neighborhood safety.

Environmental Justice: Protecting Vulnerable Communities

The Democratic Party acknowledges the disproportionate influence of environmental degradation on prone communities and is dedicated to environmental justice. It helps insurance policies that tackle environmental disparities, promote easy energy, and guard herbal resources. The birthday celebration additionally advocates for neighborhood involvement in environmental decision-making procedures and helps initiatives that prioritize the fitness and well-being of communities affected with the aid of air pollution and local weather change. By championing environmental justice, the Democratic Party ambitions to create a society the place all individuals, regardless of their socioeconomic repute or location, can experience a smooth and healthful environment.

Civic Engagement and Voting Rights: Strengthening Democracy for All

The Democratic Party believes in the crucial significance of civic engagement and defending balloting rights. It helps insurance policies that increase get right of entry to to the ballot, minimize obstacles to voter participation, and promote truthful and invulnerable elections. The celebration additionally advocates for marketing campaign finance reform to minimize the affect of cash in politics and helps initiatives that support democratic institutions. By championing civic engagement and vote casting rights, the Democratic Party ambitions to create a democracy that is inclusive, transparent, and consultant of the various voices inside the nation.

Conclusion:

The Democratic Party's dedication to fairness and social justice is a cornerstone of its imaginative and prescient for a honest and inclusive society. Through insurance policies and initiatives aimed at addressing systemic inequalities, merchandising social cohesion, and developing a society that upholds the values of equality, fairness, and chance for all Americans, the celebration strives to construct a better and extra simply nation. While challenges persist, the Democratic Party's dedication to making sure fairness and social justice displays its unwavering dedication to developing a society that leaves no one in the back of and upholds the ideas upon which the United States was once founded.

www.ingramcontent.com/pod-product-compliance
Lightning Source LLC
Chambersburg PA
CBHW072332270726
48658CB00016B/2369